Advent Activities for Preschool Children

LET'S GET READY FOR

St. Louis de Montfort
11441 Hague Rd.
Fishers, IN 46038

W9-AHK-846

CONTENTS

Acknowledgments

Typographer: Connie Helgeson-Moen
Editors: Beth Ann Gaede, Louise Lystig

Scripture quotations are from NRSV—New Revised Standard Version Bible, copyright © 1989 Division of Christian Education of the National Council of the Churches of Christ in the USA, used by permission; RSV—Revised Standard Version of the Bible, copyright © 1946, 1952, 1971 Division of Christian Education of the National Council of the Churches of Christ in the USA, used by permission; TEV—Good News Bible, Today's English Version, copyright © 1966, 1971, 1976 American Bible Society, used by permission.

ISBN 0-8066-2662-3

Let's Get Ready for Christmas is a collection of Advent activities that will help three- to five-year-old children and their parents and families, teachers, or other helpers explore the meaning of Advent. The Bible stories and related activities give enthusiastic little hands plenty of opportunities to get ready for Jesus' birthday.

The book is divided into four themes, one for each week of Advent: Let's prepare!, Let's serve!, Let's give!, and Let's celebrate! Each theme begins with an introductory page of information about how to present the theme to preschool children and how the theme ties into the Christmas story, a Bible verse, and a fun activity for adults and children to do together.

You will find a variety of activities for each week of Advent. The first theme-related activity is always a Bible story. The remaining ones further develop the theme. Begin each week with the Bible story activity. Then skim the week's activities and choose one or more that you and your child would enjoy and can comfortably manage.

The activities will stimulate lots of conversation, which is where the real learning takes place. Suggested dialog is provided to help you get started, but do not worry about trying to follow the printed dialog exactly. Let your conversation with your child be easy and natural.

Look for Graymouse within the border on each page. She is a furry little creature who is getting ready for Christmas. Your preschool child will delight in finding her in a different location within every border. When your child finds Graymouse, talk about how she is getting ready for Christmas. You also can make a Graymouse ornament as described on page 28.

The color for Advent used in this book is blue. Throughout the history of the church, various colors, including combinations of white, purple, and pink have been used during Advent. An ancient tradition that is being used more commonly is the use of the color blue to symbolize hope.

This book may be used in several settings, such as home, Sunday school or other church settings, or day school. Use your own creativity to adapt suggested activities to suit your child, setting, budget, or the time you have available. If you use this resource outside the home, some activities will need to be adjusted. Consider inviting youth, seniors, and other adult members of your congregation to get ready for Christmas in a lively intergenerational event.

dvent means "coming." During Advent we prepare with hope and expectation for the coming of Jesus. We remember Jesus' coming as an infant on that first Christmas Day. We rejoice in Jesus' coming among us in the present. We anticipate the time when Jesus will come again.

Introduce Advent to your preschool child as a time to prepare for Jesus' birthday. Find a photo album that shows how parents, grandparents, and great-grandparents throughout the years have prepared for and celebrated Christ's birth. Point out family and church traditions such as sharing a special meal on Christmas Eve, making food baskets for needy families, participating in a church Christmas program, and caroling. Talk about ways your child would like to help your family prepare for Christmas.

Read the story of Jesus' birth to your child from Luke 2:1-20. Explain words that might be difficult to understand. If possible, read the story from a simpler Bible translation such as Today's English Version, also called the Good News Bible, or the New Revised Standard Version Bible. Encourage your child to retell the story. Talk together about Mary's feelings of surprise and happiness when she learned she would become Jesus' mother, and the angels' feelings of joy as they sang about the birth of God's Son. Imagine the shepherds' feelings of fear and wonder when they first heard the angel's words, and their feelings of great happiness after seeing baby Jesus.

The Bible verse for the first week in Advent is "Prepare the way of the Lord" (Mark 1:3 NRSV). Read the verse to your child. Then say, "Jesus' birth was not really a surprise to God's people. God promised to send his Son, Jesus, to the world to teach us about God's love. But the people didn't know when Jesus would come. They watched. They waited. And they got ready for Jesus' coming by trying to do what God want them to do. God also promised to send a messenger to help the people prepare for Jesus' coming. This messenger's name was John. John told the people to prepare the way of the Lord."

During the first week in Advent pray this Bible verse litany with your child. Try singing the Bible verse response.

Jesus Is Coming

LEADER: Advent means coming. Jesus is coming.

ALL: Prepare the way of the Lord!

LEADER: Let's wait together. Let's sing while waiting.

ALL: Prepare the way of the Lord!

LEADER: Let's read the Bible. Let's pray together.

ALL: Prepare the way of the Lord!

LEADER: Let's help each other to welcome God's Son.

ALL: Prepare the way of the Lord! Amen

Pre - pare___ the way of the Lord!___ A - men

You will need:

your child's baby album or other pictures of babies
your child's favorite baby toy or blanket

Locate the photo album of your child's baby pictures, or refer to other pictures of babies, perhaps cut out of magazines. Sit with your child and talk about each photo, what a wonderful event it was when your child entered your family, and how your child fills your life with joy. Talk about the long wait and how you prepared for your child's arrival. Tell some memorable and silly stories about things your child did as a baby. Sing your child's favorite lullaby. Find your child's favorite baby toy or blanket. Help your child recognize that the arrival of a baby brings great happiness into a family.

Say, "Families must wait a long time for babies to be born. How do they get ready?" (Possible answers include: *visit the doctor, set up a crib, and buy diapers and bottles.* Your child might come up with some surprising answers.)

"Will you help me tell a Bible story? It's about a couple named Elizabeth and Zechariah. (Have your child repeat their names.) Elizabeth and Zechariah always wanted children. But they were old, too old to have children. Then they had a happy surprise. We're going to use our faces to show how they felt during different times in the story."

 HAPPY   SAD   SURPRISED   AFRAID

Zechariah and Elizabeth loved God. They prayed to God to give them children, but they had none. This made them 😟 sometimes.

Zechariah worked in the temple, a place to worship God. One day when Zechariah was inside the temple an angel of God appeared to him. Zechariah was 😮 and 😨 . But the angel said, "Do not be 😨 , your prayer has been heard. Your wife, Elizabeth, will have a baby and you will name him John. John will make you very 😀 . Many people will be 😀 because John will help the people get ready for Jesus.

Zechariah asked the angel, "How can I be sure of this? I am an old man and my wife is old, too."

The angel answered, "I am Gabriel. God sent me to tell you this 😀 news. But because you did not believe my words, you will not be able to speak until the day this happens."

When Zechariah left the temple he could not speak. He made signs with his hands instead.

Elizabeth was very 😀 when she learned what the angel promised. And the angel's words came true. Soon Elizabeth was expecting a baby. Elizabeth and Zechariah were very 😀 as they prepared for baby John's birth.

When baby John was born, Elizabeth and Zechariah were very 😀 . Their relatives and neighbors were 😮 and 😀 .

The people asked Zechariah what the baby's name would be. He wrote, "His name is John," and then Zechariah could talk again. Zechariah was so 😀 that he sang a song of praise to God.

You will need:

four blue candles (keep several extras on hand)
four stable candle holders
evergreen branches (real or artificial)
36 inches of sturdy, flexible wire
green wire twisters or florist's wire
a ring

Bring out the four blue candles, and let your child examine them. Ask, "What color are these candles? *(Blue.)* Blue is the church color for Advent. What else is blue? *(Sky, sea, blueberries, flowers, and household items.)* Let's find some blue things." Have a blue hunt. Find familiar blue household objects such as dishes, clothing, toys, toothpaste, and combs. Say, "Whenever we see something blue we can remember that it's Advent, the time we get ready for Jesus' birth."

Return to the blue candles. Ask, "How many blue candles do we have? (Count them together.) The four blue candles remind us of the four weeks we wait for Jesus' birth." Place the candles in candle holders.

Pick up the length of wire and bend it into a circle, twisting the ends together. Ask, "What shape is this? *(A circle.)*" Hold up a ring and ask, "What shape is this? *(A circle.)*" Slip the ring onto your child's finger. Let your child examine the ring while you ask, "Where does the circle begin? Where does the circle end? *(It doesn't have a beginning or an end.)* The circle reminds us of God's love. God's love doesn't begin or end either. God *always* loves us."

Hold up the evergreen branches. Say, "These branches come from a pine tree or an evergreen tree. Do pine trees lose their needles in the fall? *(No.)* Their needles stay green all year long. Evergreen branches remind us that God's love is always with us, in winter, spring, summer, and fall." Let your child help you wind the branches around the wire circle. Secure the branches with wire twisters or green florist's wire. Inside the wreath evenly space out the four blue candles. Let your child choose a place to display the Advent wreath.

ADVENT RHYME

Say the appropriate rhyme with your child as you light one, two, three, or four candles during the four weeks of Advent.

WEEK 1

One blue candle burning.
Three blue candles left to say,
"Three weeks to get ready
And wait for Jesus' birthday."

WEEK 2

Two blue candles burning.
Two blue candles left to say,
"Two weeks to get ready
And wait for Jesus' birthday."

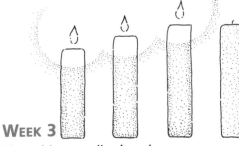

WEEK 3

Three blue candles burning.
One blue candle left to say,
"One week to get ready
And wait for Jesus' birthday."

WEEK 4

Four blue candles burning.
Four sparkling lights shine to say,
"Jesus' birthday's almost here.
Oh, merry, merry Christmas Day!"

You will need:

one 9-by-12-inch piece of blue felt
sharp scissors, glitter pen
blue thread, needle
four small jingle bells
sequins, white glue
measuring tape or ruler
paper and pencil

With your child, walk around your home and choose a place to display your doorhanger. Measure the doorknob at its largest point. Cut the piece of blue felt in half, making two 6-by-9-inch pieces. On a sheet of 6-by-9-inch paper you or your child may make a pattern for the shape of the doorhanger. Include a circular opening a little larger than the size of the doorknob and place it about one inch from the top. Cut out the pattern. Then, trace it onto one piece of felt and cut out the doorhanger shape. Repeat this for the second piece of felt, and glue the two matching felt shapes together to make the doorhanger sturdy.

Use a glitter pen to print the words *Jesus Is Coming* or a similar message chosen by your child on the doorhanger. Let your child arrange and glue on sequins. Decorate the shape using a combination of the glitter pen and sequins. You can teach about patterns by alternating large and small sequins. Set the doorhanger aside to dry, keeping it flat. After it is dry, thread a needle with blue thread, and attach the four jingle bells separately along the bottom of the doorhanger using varying lengths of thread.

Display the doorhanger in the spot you chose earlier. Ask your child, "What does *Advent* mean? *(Coming.)* Who is coming? *(Jesus.)* Why is our doorhanger blue? *(Blue is the color for Advent.)* How many bells does it have? (Count the bells together.) Why do we have four bells? *(During Advent we wait four weeks for Jesus' birthday.)*" Compliment your child as you admire your doorhanger. Open and close the door several times to hear the bells ring.

"OH, CLAP AND BE JOYFUL"

Take a listening walk around your home. Encourage your child to name different sounds you hear such as a clock ticking, water running, cars passing by, and birds calling. Ask, "What are some sounds we hear as we are getting ready for Christmas?" *(Choirs practicing Christmas songs, bells ringing, friendly voices, and Christmas music in stores are possible answers.)*

One way we can get ready for Christmas is by learning a new song about Jesus' birth. Learn this happy Christmas song with your child. You may sing the first stanza when you light the candles on your Advent wreath during the first and second weeks. Add the second stanza for the third week and the third stanza for the fourth week.

1. Oh, clap and be __ joy-ful, Lord Je-sus loves you. God loves us and sent him, it __ rea-ly is true. Oh, clap and be __ joy-ful, we'll __ sing it for you. God loves us, and through us God loves oth-ers, too.

2. A - way in a __ man-ger, no __ crib for his bed, the __ lit-tle Lord Je-sus laid __ down his sweet head; the stars in the __ sky __ looked down where he lay, the __ lit-tle Lord Je-sus, a - sleep on the hay.

3. The shep-herds were watch-ing out __ un-der the sky. Their sheep lay there sleep-ing on __ hill-sides near - by. An an-gel came to them: "Fear __ not," he did say, "for __ God sent a Sa-vior for __ you on this day."

Words: Traditional, st. 2; Hildegard Kuse, st. 1 and 3, copyright © 1978 Augsburg Publishing House   Music: William J. Kirkpatrick

You will need:

one unlined index card, small box
marker, one button for each player

Cut the index card into four game cards. Write 1, 2, 3, or 4 on each card. Place the cards face down inside the box. Use the small buttons for game pieces.

To play the game: Place game pieces on the "start" square. Have your child draw a card from the box. Name the number and help your child move that number of spaces on the game board. Do or pretend to do what is described on the space. Return the card, face down, to the box. Then it is the second player's turn. Play continues until all players reach the crèche scene. Whoever finishes first gives his or her turns to the other players.

Or create an Advent Joy Jar. Let your child draw something related to the activity on one side of a small piece of paper, and someone can print the idea on the other side. Choose one activity a day.

START

LIGHT 1 CANDLE ON THE ADVENT WREATH

SING A CHRISTMAS SONG

SHARE A SMILE

TELL THE CHRISTMAS STORY

OPEN A DOOR ON AN ADVENT CALENDAR

MAKE A CHRISTMAS GIFT

SET OUT A CRÈCHE

GO AHEAD 1 SPACE

GO BACK 1 SPACE

TELL SOMEONE, "I LOVE YOU"

READ THE BIBLE

HELP SOMEONE IN YOUR FAMILY

MAKE A CHRISTMAS CARD

TAKE A WALK AND ENJOY GOD'S CREATION GIFTS

HANG A CHRISTMAS WREATH ON YOUR DOOR

LIGHT 2 CANDLES ON THE ADVENT WREATH

HUG SOMEONE

PRAY

GO AHEAD 2 SPACES

INVITE SOMEONE TO COME TO CHURCH WITH YOU

MAKE WRAPPING PAPER

LIGHT CANDLES 3 ON THE ADVENT WREATH

MAKE A CHRISTMAS ORNAMENT

LIGHT CANDLES 4 ON THE ADVENT WREATH

GIVE GIFTS TO YOUR FAMILY

TEACH A CHRISTMAS SONG TO A FRIEND

KISS SOMEONE

SEND A CHRISTMAS CARD

GO BACK 1 SPACE

DECORATE A CHRISTMAS TREE

WRAP A CHRISTMAS GIFT

BAKE CHRISTMAS COOKIES

BRING A BASKET OF FOOD TO A NEEDY FAMILY

GATHER FOOD FOR A FOOD DRIVE

SAY THANK YOU TO GOD FOR SENDING baby JESUS

PICK UP LITTER

10

hen we serve others we discover the gifts and talents that God has given us. Each one of us is blessed with gifts, gifts God wants us to use to serve humankind. During Advent teach your child that with our gifts comes the responsibility to serve each other and care for God's creation. As we get ready for Christmas we can tell the stories of Mary and Elizabeth, who served the Lord, as well as the story of Jesus, who came to teach us how to serve others.

Your child's self-esteem grows as he or she learns to do age-appropriate jobs. Some of these may be routine—like picking up toys, making the bed, matching clean socks in the laundry, picking up litter in the yard, and setting the table. Find ways to involve your child in Christmas preparations, too. Your preschool child will enjoy helping you with cooking, decorating, gathering canned goods for a food pantry, and making simple Christmas gifts. Through service to others your child will discover that he or she is a valuable person, loved by you and loved by God.

The Bible verse for the second week of Advent is "Serve the Lord with gladness!" (Psalm 100:2 RSV). Every day during the second week of Advent you may do this action rhyme with your child as a reminder that by serving others, we can prepare for Jesus' birthday.

Serve the Lord with Gladness!

Up! Down! All around!
(stretch up high on tiptoes, crouch down low, stand and open arms out wide)

Serve the Lord with gladness!
(jump twice and lift arms high overhead)

Clap your hands! Twirl around!
(clap hands twice, spin around once)

Serve the Lord with gladness!
(jump twice and lift arms high overhead)

Tiptoe high! Stomp down low!
(walk on tiptoes, then stomp feet and move like an elephant)

Serve the Lord with gladness!
(jump twice and lift arms high overhead)

Sing, "La, la!" Laugh, "Ho, ho!"
(cup hands around mouth while smiling)

Serve the Lord with gladness!
(jump twice and lift arms high overhead)

Dance, dance for a while!
(hold your child's hands and dance together)

Serve the Lord with gladness!
(jump twice and lift arms high overhead)

Hug someone! Give a smile!
(get on your knees and smile as you hug your standing child)

Serve the Lord with gladness!
(jump twice and lift arms high overhead)

You will need:

three paper plates, three craft sticks
masking tape, glue, scissors
crayons or markers
fabric scraps, yarn

Help your child make three paper plate puppets for a Bible story puppet show. Write one of the following names on the back of a paper plate: Mary, Gabriel, or Elizabeth. Use crayons or markers to draw the facial features for the three characters. Keep in mind that Mary was a very young woman and Elizabeth was old. Let your child choose fabric to make headdresses for Mary and Elizabeth. Glue in place. Add yarn for hair. Use your imaginations to create Gabriel, the angel. After the glue has dried, make a handle for each puppet by taping a craft stick to the back of the paper plate. Before the puppet show begins, review the Bible story on page 5, connecting the characters with the puppets.

Find a stage, such as a coffee table, a sofa, or a bed. Make sure your child knows the name of each puppet. When you call out the puppet's name, your child will raise the puppet. Direct the puppet's actions while you read the story.

Mary puppet

Elizabeth puppet

Gabriel puppet

MARY: *(hold up MARY puppet)*

I lived in a small house in Nazareth. I was engaged to be married to a man named Joseph. Joseph was a carpenter. He built furniture out of wood. One day I had a surprising visitor, an angel named Gabriel. Gabriel was God's messenger.

(add GABRIEL puppet)

GABRIEL: Greetings, you who are loved by God! God is with you.

MARY: *(aside)* I was afraid and troubled by the angel's visit. I wondered what his words meant.

GABRIEL: Do not be afraid, Mary. God loves you. You will give birth to a son. You will name him Jesus. Jesus will be great and will be called the Son of the Most High God.

(remove GABRIEL puppet)

MARY: I was very surprised by the angel Gabriel's message. I wanted to share this happy news with my cousin Elizabeth. She was going to have a baby, too. I quickly packed and hurried to her home in the country.

(add ELIZABETH puppet)

MARY: Greetings, Elizabeth!

ELIZABETH: Blessed are you among women, and blessed is the baby you will have. As soon as I heard your voice, the baby inside me jumped for joy. Blessed are you, Mary, who has believed the angel's words from God.

MARY: Praise God for choosing me to be God's servant. God has done great things for me.

(remove ELIZABETH puppet)

MARY: I stayed with Elizabeth for about three months and then returned home.

You will need:

one sheet of sturdy poster board
scissors, single-hole punch
green construction paper
paper, pencil, markers, or crayons
tape or glue, tack, hammer
optional: red construction paper,
 fabric bow, tiny Christmas ornaments

Plan to do this activity with the whole family. Set aside a time to sit down together. Explain that one way we can prepare for Christmas is by serving others as Jesus taught us to do. List ways your family can serve each other at home, serve at church, and serve in the community. (For possible community service projects, see page 24.)

Cut a 4-inch thick ring as large as possible from a sheet of poster board. Punch a hole in the top of the ring to hang it. Have all family members trace outlines of one of their hands on pieces of green construction paper and cut out the tracings. Assist the younger children as needed. Then print on each tracing one way that person has served. Even the youngest children can serve through their smiles, hugs, songs, and kisses. Use tape or glue to attach the hand tracings to the ring. Try to have each family member add one hand tracing every day.

Continue this activity throughout Advent. Your preschool child will have fun watching the wreath become covered with "greens." Several days before Christmas, decorate the wreath with red construction paper berries, a bright fabric bow, and tiny Christmas ornaments. Enjoy the wreath throughout the Christmas season.

You will need:

12-by-18-inch sheets of construction paper
clear adhesive paper, scissors
crayons or markers, single-hole punch
thin colorful fabric ribbon, tape

Say to your child, "Let's make an Advent placemat. What color should it be?" (Remember that blue is the church color for Advent.) Hold up a sheet of construction paper in the color your child chose and ask, "What shape is this paper?" *(A rectangle.)* What can we draw on this paper to remind us of Jesus' birthday? (Some possible answers include: *baby Jesus in a manger, shepherds, Mary, candles burning, angels singing, and happy faces.)"*

Invite your child to draw pictures about celebrating Jesus' birthday. If your child can print, have him or her copy the words *Jesus loves (your child's name)* on the construction paper. Then print this prayer in a free space, as shown below.

Thank you, God, for sending Jesus to teach our 🖐🖐 to help and our ♡♡ to love. Amen.
Jesus Loves Karin

Cover the front and the back of the paper with clear adhesive paper. Use a paper punch to make holes around the edges of the placemat, spacing them about one inch apart. Wrap one end of colorful fabric ribbon with tape to make a needle. Teach your preschool child how to lace the ribbon through the holes starting at the center of the top, to make a decorative border. (Don't worry if the lacing isn't perfect.) Tie the two ends of ribbon into a bow.

You and your child may make an Advent placemat for each family member. At meals pray the prayer written on your child's placemat to give thanks for God's gift of Jesus and as a reminder to serve others.

You will need:

bathrobes, towels
fabric sashes, headbands, sandals
several of the following foods: pita bread, olives,
   grape juice, figs, grapes, cheeses, apricots,
   cucumbers, walnuts, almonds, yogurt, raisins

Preschool children love to pretend. Boys and girls mimic the daily activities in their homes such as sweeping the floor, vacuuming, cooking, and caring for the baby.

One way we can serve others is by preparing food for them. Work with your preschool child to prepare a meal much like what Mary or Jesus would have eaten. Write down the foods listed on this page. Then take your child grocery shopping to gather some of these foods people would have eaten in biblical times.

Show your child how to prepare a simple meal by using a table knife to slice soft cheese and to cut the pita bread into bite-size pieces. Attractively arrange the foods on a tray.

Before eating, invite all family members to dress as Mary and Jesus might have dressed. Put on bathrobes tied with colorful sashes at the waist. Cover the top of everyone's head with a lightweight towel or large scarf and secure around the top of the head with a headband or cord. Wear sandals or go barefoot.

Let your child invite everyone to the meal. Then say, "Let's pretend that we are living long, long ago in a house next door to Mary, Jesus' mother. These are some of the kinds of foods we would eat." Invite your preschool child to lead the family in a table prayer.

While you're eating, talk about how people prepared these foods during Mary's time:

Bread—The grain was sifted to remove small stones and stalks and ground into flour with a handmill. The flour was mixed with water and yeast, then the dough was left to rise. The loaves were baked in clay ovens.

Grapes—Grapes were eaten fresh, dried in the sun to make raisins, or pressed into grape juice. To make grape juice, people carried big baskets of grapes and dumped them into a big tub. Barefooted people stamped on the grapes. The grape juice drained into a lower tub. Most of this juice was made into wine.

Cheese—Cheese is made from milk. The cheesemaker adds special ingredients to milk to make it into curds. The curds are pressed together into cheese. Cheese keeps a long time without spoiling before it is eaten.

Olives—Olives grew on trees all around Nazareth. The olives were eaten or pressed into olive oil. People used the olive oil to cook and, by burning it in small clay pots, to light their homes.

You will need:

- two sheets of 9-by-12-inch white or pastel construction paper
- single-hole punch, colorful ribbon or yarn
- photograph of your child
- crayons or markers, glue

Many preschool children are fascinated by small books, especially ones they have made themselves. Help your child make this book as a reminder of ways he or she can serve at home.

Fold the sheets of construction paper in half to make 6-by-9-inch pages. Nest one sheet inside the other sheet. Punch one hole near the top of the folded edge and one near the bottom, punching through all four layers. Thread colorful ribbon or yarn through the holes and tie in a bow. In small numerals, number each page 1 through 8.

Page 1: Glue the photograph of your child to the front of the book. Print *My Helping Hands* above the photo. Let your child draw a colorful frame around the photo and print his or her name below it.

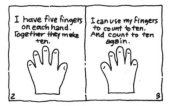

Page 2: Use a crayon or marker to trace around your child's left hand. Let your child add details such as fingernails, freckles, and rings. On the top of the page print *I have five little fingers on each hand. Together they make ten.*

Page 3: Trace around your child's right hand. Let your child use his or her imagination to add details. On the top of the page print *I can use my fingers to count to ten. And count to ten again.*

Page 4: On the top of the page print *God gave me hands for helping. God gave me hands—one, two! Now here are ten helping things my little hands can do.* Print the numerals 1 and 2 along the outer edge of the paper. Talk to your child about two ways your child can help. Let your child draw a picture of these helping ways beside the numbers. Label your child's pictures. Here are some suggestions of ways your child can help: set the table, pick up toys, match clean socks in the laundry, play with a younger child, hold the dust pan, dust, water plants, feed pets, turn off lights, open frozen food containers, stir pudding or cake batter or muffin dough, put groceries away on lower shelves, and pick up litter in the yard.

Page 5: Print the numerals 3 and 4 along the outer edge and let your child draw two more ways to help.

Page 6:
Continue with numerals 5 and 6.

Page 7:
Continue with numerals 7 and 8.

Page 8: Finish with numerals 9 and 10. At the bottom of the page write *Thank you, God, for giving me hands to help. Amen.*

As you read this book with your child, count to 10, talk about all the ways your child can help, and tell your preschool child how proud you are of his or her accomplishments. Whenever your child helps, thank him or her with a big hug and loving words. Remind your child that helping is a great way to get ready for Christmas.

uring Advent your preschool child will surely notice people everywhere emphasizing giving and receiving gifts. Your child might see or hear special appeals to give to people in need. Often young children think that Christmas is the time to receive lots and lots of presents from Santa. The celebration of Jesus' birth might recede into the background, like an afterthought. But Jesus' birthday and Santa Claus don't have to pull your child's understanding of Christmas in opposite directions, because both have to do with giving.

Preschool children learn about the world through their senses. A pretty package to hold, shake, and admire is more real to them than the story of a baby born in a stable. The anticipation of opening that pretty package is more real than the anticipation of Jesus' birthday. The activities suggested for this week are chosen to help your preschool child experience one thing: We give each other Christmas gifts to remember God's greatest gift of all, a gift for all people—Jesus.

You can begin by telling your child, "Gifts sometimes come in pretty packages." Hug your child as you say, "Here is another kind of gift we can give." Kiss your child as you say, "This is a gift we can give, too. Last week we discovered many ways we can serve others. Whenever we help someone we are giving them a gift. During Advent we get ready for God's greatest gift to us—Jesus. At Christmas we give gifts to each other to remember God's gift of baby Jesus."

The Bible verse for the third week of Advent is "For God so loved the world that he gave his only Son" (John 3:16 NRSV). God gave us Jesus and God gives us life. God also entrusts us to care for God's gift of creation. To remind your child of all of the ways we experience God's gifts through our five senses, say this action prayer every day during the third week of Advent:

 Thank you, God for giving us
(fold hands in prayer)

 hands to serve people in need,
(open hands, palms up)

 eyes to see signs of your love,
(point to eyes, cross arms across chest)

 ears to hear happy voices singing,
(point to ears, cup hands around mouth)

 noses to smell goodies baking in the oven,
(point to nose, pat stomach)

 mouths to taste the food you have given us,
(point to mouth, pat stomach)

 and hearts to share your love.
(gently squeeze your child's hands)

Amen

You will need:

four small wooden blocks, baby doll
box large enough to place the doll inside
white dish towels or strips from an old sheet
several pillows

Say to your child, "Let's act out the Christmas story, the story about the time when baby Jesus was born. Do you remember Jesus' mother's name? *(Mary.)* Mary was going to marry Joseph, a carpenter. God sent an angel to tell Joseph about the special baby Mary would have. Our story starts when it is almost time for Mary's baby to be born."

The king ordered all people to go back to the towns they came from to be counted. *(Hold up the fingers on both of your hands for your child to count.)* The king wanted to know how many people lived in his land. Joseph came from a town called Bethlehem, so Mary and Joseph had to travel to Bethlehem to be counted by the king.

Mary climbed up onto their donkey. *(Sit down on chairs.)* The donkey's hooves made a clip-clop, clip clop sound as Joseph led him along the dusty road. *(Slowly sway from side to side as you hit two wooden blocks together in a clip-clop rhythm.)* Mary and Joseph travelled all day. *(Continue swaying and hitting the blocks together.)* Finally they reached Bethlehem.

Joseph stopped at the inn and knocked on the door. *(Together knock on one of the doors in your home.)*

The innkeeper opened the door and said, "The inn is full."

"My wife is going to have a baby soon," said Joseph. "Is there another place where we can rest for the night?"

"You may rest in the stable," answered the innkeeper.

Joseph and Mary travelled down the road to the stable. *(Sit on chairs and sway from side to side while hitting the wooden blocks together.)*

Inside the stable Joseph gathered the straw into a bed for Mary. *(Arrange the pillows into a bed.)* Then he helped Mary get down from the donkey. Mary rested in the straw bed. *(Both of you lie down on the pillows.)*

That night baby Jesus was born. *(Sit up and let your child hold the doll.)* Mary wrapped him in clean cloths. *(Wrap the doll in the cloths or towels.)* Mary held baby Jesus and softly sang to him. She thought, "The angel's words have come true. I am holding baby Jesus in my arms."

Mary said to Joseph, "Joseph, we have no cradle for baby Jesus."

Joseph answered, "Let's put baby Jesus in this manger. It is filled with clean straw."

Mary placed baby Jesus in the manger. *(Place the doll in the box.)* Mary and Joseph were very happy because Jesus was born. *(Smile as you look at the doll.)*

A CRÈCHE

You will need:

matchbox or other tiny box
large shoebox with lid
assorted small sizes of wood scraps (you may substitute sturdy cardboard or wooden dowels for the wood scraps)
sand paper, glue, tiny black beads
tan felt, scraps of fabric or felt
scissors, straw or yellow yarn
magazine pictures of animals (optional)
fine-point markers, chenille craft stems
cotton balls, brown paper bags

Plan to make this project throughout the week, perhaps doing one of the steps each day. (Note: If you use cardboard instead of wood scraps for the figures, cut a piece of cardboard 3 inches wide and as long as the height of the figure. Fold the cardboard lengthwise in thirds and tape the long edges together to make a form for a free-standing figure.)

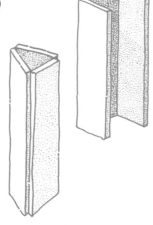

Step 1—The stable

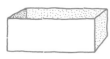

Cut five pieces of a brown paper bag to fit the inside sides and bottom of the shoebox. Glue in place. The bottom will become the back wall of the stable when the box is turned on its side.

Draw pictures of cows, a donkey, doves, and sheep on the piece of brown paper you cut for the bottom of the box. Or cut out pictures of animals from magazines and glue them to the brown paper. Turn the box on its side so the animals are standing up. Use brown or yellow markers to draw straw on the floor.

Step 2—The manger and baby Jesus

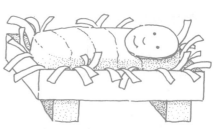

Glue small pieces of yellow yarn or straw to the inside of the matchbox. Find two 1-by-1½-inch wood scraps. Use sandpaper to smooth the pieces. Glue the two pieces to the bottom of the matchbox to form legs for the manger.

Find a tiny narrow wood scrap that fits inside the matchbox. This will become the baby Jesus figure. Sand it until it is smooth. Cut out a small circle of tan felt for the face. Glue on two tiny black beads for eyes. Use markers to add rosy cheeks, a little nose, and a smile. Glue the face to the wood piece. To make the swaddling clothes, wrap the wooden piece with strips of white felt or fabric and glue in place.

Step 3—Mary and Joseph

Use a rectangular scrap of wood five inches high for Mary and about six inches high for Joseph. Sand the pieces. Cut tan felt circles for faces, glue on black bead eyes, and add features with markers.

For their garments wrap colorful fabric around the wooden pieces and glue in place. Choose contrasting fabric for the headdresses. Glue in place and tie yarn around them. For Joseph, add a beard using yarn or brown fabric. From tan felt cut out four small hands. Glue a pair of hands to the front of each figure, placing them near the outer edges.

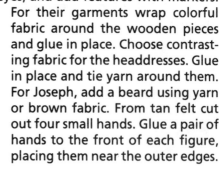

Step 4—Shepherds

Use three rectangular scraps of wood—one six inches high, one five inches high, and one three inches high. Follow the directions for making Mary and Joseph. Use the 3-inch scrap to make a shepherd boy. Bend the three brown chenille craft stems into staffs. Adjust the lengths of the staffs to match the heights of the figures. Glue in place.

Step 6—Angel

Find a piece of wood about eight inches high, wide at the base and narrow at the top. Sand smooth. Cut out a round face from tan felt and glue it near the top of the wood. Add black bead eyes, rosy cheeks, and a smiling face. Then use your imaginations to make a beautiful gown, perhaps using white netting, lace, eyelet, or satin. Decorate with a glitter pen or by gluing on sequins.

Encourage your child to play freely with the figures while retelling the Christmas story. The figures can be easily stored by placing them in the shoebox, adding the lid, and securing with a rubber band. You and your child can look forward to setting up the crèche Christmas after Christmas.

Step 5—Sheep

Use three or four rectangular scraps of wood about 1-by-2-inches each. Sand smooth. Cover most of the wood (except the bottom) with cotton balls. Cut out a black felt or fabric triangle and glue in place for the face. Add bead eyes and two tiny strips of black felt or fabric for ears.

21

CREATION GIFTS

You will need:

9-by-12-inch sheet of cardboard, glue, fine sandpaper
green, blue, and white fabric scraps or construction paper
crayons or markers, yellow button
small photographs of all family members

On a sunny day, take your child outdoors. Look up at the sky and ask, "What color is the sky? *(Blue.)* Is the sky big or little? *(Big.)* Who made the sky? *(God.)*" Examine a tree or shrub. Touch its bark and ask, "How does the bark of this tree feel? *(Probably rough.)*" Have your child stand next to the tree and decide if he or she is taller or shorter than the tree. Ask, "Who made this tree? *(God.)*"

If an evergreen tree or bush is nearby, pluck one of the needles, break it in half, and enjoy its fragrance with your child. Ask, "Who made this tree that smells so good? *(God.)*" Stand quietly for a moment and name sounds you hear. Listen for wind blowing through the trees, birds chirping, and your own breathing. Ask, "Who made the birds? *(God.)* Who made us? *(God.)* God made the sky, the wind, the trees, and the birds. God gave us the world to care for and enjoy. Advent is a time to remember that."

To remind your child of creation gifts, help your child make this creation collage. For the sky cut out strips of light blue fabric or construction paper and glue to a piece of cardboard. Add white or green fabric or paper strips for the ground, depending upon whether you have snow or grass. Glue on a yellow button for the sun.

Help your child cut out a tree trunk from fine sandpaper. Glue on the sheet of cardboard. Cut out small pieces of green felt or fabric to glue above and around the trunk to make an evergreen tree. On a sheet of white paper have your child use bright markers or crayons to draw several tiny birds. Cut out the birds and place them on the collage.

Find photographs of family members. Cut out the figures and glue them to the picture. If you live where it gets cold in the winter, you might cut out a tiny coat for each family member and glue the coats to the photos.

Display the collage in your child's room. Every night before your child goes to bed, look at the creation collage together. Feel the rough tree trunk and the smooth leaves. Admire the coats on the photos of your family members. Then pray together, "Thank you, God, for all of your gifts to us, especially baby Jesus. Amen."

You will need:

12 colorful sheets of 9-by-12-inch construction paper, sandpaper, white typing paper, scissors, single-hole punch, yarn or ribbon, photograph of your child, glue, markers, watercolor paints, crayons, fabric scraps, ribbon, cotton balls, glitter, plastic straw

Plan to do this project over the course of several days, perhaps completing two or three pages each day. Copy and enlarge the pattern for the calendar on this page to 8-by-6-inches. Make 12 copies of the pattern on a copy machine. Cut out the 12 copies and glue each one to the bottom half of a sheet of construction paper. Write the name of the month and the numbers of the days of each month on each page. If your child can write, let him or her write the numbers.

Here are some suggestions for decorating each calendar page. Use these ideas, or substitute your child's ideas.

January—Have your child draw and cut out three white circles of different sizes. Glue to the page to make a snowman. Add snowflakes by gluing on tiny paper circles made with a paper punch. Use markers to add a face and other details.

February—Glue your child's photo on the left side, a big heart in the middle, and the word *YOU* on the right side.

March—Cut a kite out of a fabric scrap and glue on the page. Draw the kite string. Draw a shorter string and add tiny bows for the kite's tail.

April—Glue cotton-ball clouds at the very top of the page. Have your child use a blue marker or blue watercolor paint to make raindrops. Find room for a rainbow, too.

May—Draw a row of colorful flowers.

June—Let your child draw a beach scene. Glue on a strip of sandpaper for the beach. Glue thin wisps of cotton for the clouds. Add people swimming, building sand castles, and sunbathing.

July—Drop paint onto the paper. Use a straw to blow it into fireworks patterns. Add glitter.

August—Draw all kinds of fish, starfish, crabs, shellfish, and plants. Cut out the shapes and glue to blue construction paper to make an underwater scene.

September—Make a big yellow school bus. Draw a different face in each window.

October—Draw a big, bare tree trunk and branches. Use a paper punch to make circles of red, orange, and yellow construction paper. Glue to the tree and near the base of the tree for fall leaves.

November—Trace around your child's opened hand. Turn the hand tracing into a turkey by adding a beak and wattle to the thumb and adding legs. Have your child color it.

December—Have your child draw baby Jesus in a manger.

To finish the calendar, punch three holes across the top of each page—one in the center and one near each end. Tie the pages together with yarn or ribbon through the two outer holes. Use a small hook or tack to hang the calendar through the center hole.

SUNDAY	MONDAY	TUESDAY	WEDNESDAY	THURSDAY	FRIDAY	SATURDAY

SHARING CHRISTMAS JOY

During Advent, many churches and communities donate items to organizations that distribute Christmas gifts to needy people. Jesus' birth in a stable reminds us of the needs and pain that might be part of our lives, even at this happy time. You and your child can celebrate Christmas together by contributing to one of these organizations or by following one of these suggestions:

1. Look for stores or shopping malls that have a Christmas tree decorated with paper ornaments that include the names of children, their ages, and the sizes of clothing or other gifts they would like. Choose an ornament for a child the same age as your preschool child, and help your child pick out a gift.

2. Bake Christmas cookies and give them to guests at a shelter for homeless people.

3. Purchase a tabletop Christmas tree and some small ornaments for a person who is homebound. You and your child can help this person decorate the tree.

4. Address Christmas cards for someone who could use the help. Your child could attach stamps and return address labels and seal the envelopes.

5. Wash, inspect, and repair as needed good used toys and clothes and give them to an organization that will distribute them to families in your community.

6. Gather food for a food pantry or make a Christmas goody basket for an agency that helps needy families.

7. Sing Christmas songs for residents in a care facility.

The celebration of Christmas doesn't truly begin until Christmas Day. But you and your child can prepare for the celebration during this last week of Advent, much as you would get ready for a birthday party or other festive occasion. During this week remind your child that the joy of Christmas is centered on the birth of Jesus, God's promised Son.

The week before Christmas might be a period of almost unbearable excitement and anticipation for your preschool child. It's often a time of rushing and last minute preparations for adults. Holiday stress can spoil Christmas preparations and celebrations for children and adults. And for those who are already feeling sad or lonely, holiday excitement can intensify the feelings. To help you and your child find peace amidst the clatter and chatter, set aside time to try some of these respites:

● Snuggle together in your favorite chair and read the Christmas story. Then let your child "read" the story to you. Read other favorite books, too.

● Admire your Christmas tree. If you have lights on the tree, turn on the lights and turn off the household lights. Talk about your child's favorite color or favorite ornament, and tell your child about funny and meaningful incidents from past Christmases.

● Look through the Christmas cards you have received. Tell your child about the people in the photographs. Line the cards up on a table. Pick favorites. Sort them into different themes such as Jesus' birth, humor, nostalgia, Santa, and nature. Explain that Christmas cards are gifts we give to others to celebrate God's gift of Jesus.

● Take an evening walk. Look at the stars. Feel the breeze blow on your cheeks. Point out Christmas decorations and Christmas trees in your neighborhood.

The Bible verse for the fourth week in Advent is "This very day in David's town your Savior was born—Christ the Lord!" (Luke 2:11 TEV). Read the verse to your child. Then say, "After baby Jesus was born, an angel told shepherds about his birth. The angel said, 'Today in the town of David a Savior has been born to you; he is Christ the Lord.' The shepherds knew about God's promise to send Jesus. They were afraid and joyful at the same time. Could the angel's words be true? They hurried to Bethlehem to find baby Jesus, lying in a manger. Yes! God had kept the promise! God had sent Jesus. The shepherds told this happy news to everyone they met. And they returned to their sheep, singing praises to God."

Do this Christmas counting verse with your child during the last week of Advent.

Christmas count

One! Baby Jesus asleep in the manger.
One, two! Mary and Joseph, watching over the baby.
One, two, three! Shepherds who came to worship Jesus.
One, two, three, four! Sheep who followed their shepherds.
One, two, three, four, five! Angels who sang joyfully for God's Son.

Read this Bible story with your child. You read the words. Pause when you come to a picture and let your child name it.

It was the [NIGHT] when [BABY] Jesus was born. [SHEPHERDS] were watching over their [SHEEP]. Suddenly an [ANGEL] appeared and said to the [SHEPHERDS], "Do not be afraid. I bring you good news of great joy that will be for all [PEOPLE]. Today in [BETHLEHEM] a Savior has been born to you. He is Christ the Lord. This will be a sign to you. You will find a [BABY] wrapped in [CLOTHS] and lying in a [MANGER]." Suddenly the [SKY] was filled with [ANGELS]. The [ANGELS] praised God and sang, "Glory to God in the highest and on [EARTH] peace to [PEOPLE] on whom God's favor rests. Then the [ANGELS] left. The [SHEPHERDS] said to one another, "Let's go to [BETHLEHEM] and see this [BABY] which God has told us about." So the [SHEPHERDS] hurried off. They found [MARY] and [JOSEPH] and the [BABY] who was lying in the [MANGER]. The [SHEPHERDS] told everyone they saw about [BABY] Jesus, God's Son. Then they praised God for all they had seen and heard.

You will need:

red, green, white 9-by-12-inch sheets of construction paper
sequins, glitter, scraps of ribbon
stapler, glue
markers
legal-size envelopes, Christmas wrapping paper
scissors

Say to your preschool child, "We have friends and relatives who live far away from us. We can share the happiness Jesus' birthday brings us by making and mailing Christmas cards to them."

Cut the construction paper into 6-by-9-inch pieces. Fold the paper in half to make 3-by-9-inch cards that will fit inside legal-size envelopes. Let your child decorate the front of the card by gluing or stapling on tiny bows, sequins, small scraps of Christmas wrapping paper, glitter, and other fancy odds and ends you have around your home. Inside the card write a message such as "We're sending this happy card to you to share the joy Jesus' birthday brings. Merry Christmas!" After you address your cards, take your child to the post office to buy stamps and mail your Christmas cards.

Clay decorations

You will need:

1 cup flour, 1 cup salt
plastic straw, rolling pin, large bowl
cookie cutters, table knife, waxed paper
markers or watercolor paints
⅛-inch-wide fabric ribbon, scissors
clear acrylic paint or shellac, brush

Work with your child to make the clay by mixing the flour and salt with about ¼ cup warm water. Add the water slowly until the mixture reaches a bread dough texture. Knead the ball of dough until it is smooth. Roll the dough out on waxed paper to about a ¼-inch thickness. Use cookie cutters or a table knife to cut out stars, bells, angels, or other shapes you choose.

Press a plastic straw through each shape to remove a small circle of dough. In the remaining hole you will later thread and tie thin ribbon for hanging each ornament. Allow at least three days for the ornaments to dry. Carefully turn them over once a day. After they are dry, decorate both sides of the ornaments with markers or watercolor paints. Seal the surface with clear acrylic paint or shellac. Add ribbon and hang on your Christmas tree.

Wooden bead wreaths

You will need:

red and green ½- to ¾-inch-diameter
   wooden beads
½-inch-wide fabric, ribbon
masking tape, thread (gold is fun)
needle, scissors

Wrap one end of the ribbon with masking tape to make a needle. Show your child how to create a pattern by threading on two green beads, one red bead, two green beads. Continue until you have strung enough beads to make a wreath loop that is about three inches in diameter. Remove the masking tape. Tie the ribbon into a secure knot, leaving at least six inches of extra ribbon at each end. Tie the leftover ribbon into a fancy bow. Make a loop of golden thread for hanging by sewing it through the center of the bow.

Graymouse

You will need:

walnut shell half, cotton balls
three tiny black beads, scissors
scrap of imitation gray suede or felt
white glue, thread, needle
⅛-inch-wide ribbon, fabric scrap
clear acrylic paint or shellac, brush

Help your child paint the outside of the walnut shell with clear paint or shellac. From the suede cut a thin 3-inch-long pointed tail and a ⅞-inch-diameter circle. Make a pattern for the mouse's head by tracing the one on this page. Stuff the head with part of a cotton ball. Sew on the ears and black bead eyes as shown in the illustration. Glue the head and tail to opposite ends of the inside of the walnut shell.

Stuff the shell with cotton. Cut a 2-inch-diameter fabric circle. Turn the ends under and glue along the rim of the walnut shell to make Graymouse's blanket. Make a small bow from the ribbon and sew in place under the mouse's chin. Make a hanging loop by sewing an 8-inch length of thread through the fabric circle.

Baby Jesus in a manger

Follow Step 2 in the crèche activity on page 20. To hang the ornament, sew two 12-inch lengths of golden thread through the sides of the matchbox, puncturing the centers of opposite sides. Knot the four ends together. Add a loop of thread for hanging the manger.

You will need:

lightweight paper bags, want ads
used white tissue paper, food coloring
family photos, markers, crayons, glitter
red and green tempera paint, two shallow pans
eye dropper, yarn scraps, scissors, glue

As you show your child the paper bags, want ads, and white tissue paper ask, "Are these things brand new? *(No.)*" Talk about how the bag and the tissue paper were used before. Ask, "Should we throw these things in the garbage? *(Accept your child's response.)* Instead of throwing these things away, we can use them again or recycle them. All of these were made from trees, one of God's gifts to us. When we recycle, we are caring for God's creation. We are using only what we need. Let's recycle these three kinds of paper by making Christmas wrapping paper."

Paper bags

Cut the bags along one side and turn inside out. Cut off any seams. Pour a thin layer of red tempera paint in one shallow pan and green paint in another. Protect your child's clothing with an old shirt or paint smock. Show your child how to dip one hand in the red paint and the other hand in green paint. Cover the paper with red and green hand prints.

Want ads

Use markers or crayons to draw designs on top of the want ads. Teach your child about shapes by drawing red squares and green rectangles following the shape of the printed columns. You also can make red and green stripes.

Tissue paper

Place the tissue paper on a washable surface. Smooth out the wrinkles. Let your child use an eye dropper to drop red and green food coloring onto the paper. Add several drops of clear water and watch the colors spread. Allow to dry completely before removing from the surface.

Gift tags

Let your child cut out simple shapes from a paper bag. On one side of the tag, have your child glue a photo of the person the gift is for and write the word *To*. On the back of the tag, glue a photo of the person the gift is from and write the word *From*. Decorate the tags with crayons, markers, or glitter. Use a single-hole punch to make a hole in the tag. Use recycled yarn scraps to attach the tag to the gift.

You will need:

1 cup margarine

1 cup sugar

1 egg

1 tsp. vanilla

2½ cups flour

½ tsp. baking soda

pinch of salt

fruit-flavored hard candies with a hole in the middle

plastic wrap, waxed paper, cookie sheets

Ask your preschool child, "What are some things we do to get ready for a birthday party? *(Make a cake, buy presents, decorate the home, and invite guests.)* What things have we done to get ready for Jesus' birthday? *(You may have wrapped presents, decorated your home with a Christmas tree and wreath, and sent Christmas cards to celebrate Jesus' birthday.)* Now it's time to make special cookies for Christmas. And we're going to make them together."

Help your child measure and mix the margarine, sugar, eggs, and vanilla. Measure and add the flour, baking soda, and salt. Mix well. Cover the bowl with plastic wrap and chill overnight. The next day cover the work surface with waxed paper. On the waxed paper show your child how to roll a small piece of dough into a snake. Move the snake to a well-greased cookie sheet. Shape the snake into a design, leaving enclosed open spaces for the candy. Some design suggestions are stars, candles, wreaths, happy faces (fill in eye, nose, and mouth openings with candy), bells, angels, sheep, and red Christmas flowers.

Place a whole candy in each open space. If it is a small opening, add half of a candy. After the cookie sheet is filled with cookies bake them at 350 degrees for seven to eight minutes. If you have an oven with a window, your child will have fun watching the candies melt. Let the cookies cool until the candy has hardened (about five minutes). This recipe makes about two dozen cookies. It may be doubled.

Plan to give away some of your cookies as gifts. Consider a neighbor, a resident in a care facility, a homebound member of your congregation, or guests at a shelter for homeless people. Bring your preschool child with you when you deliver the cookies. Set aside time for visiting and extending Christmas greetings with whomever you choose to give the cookies.

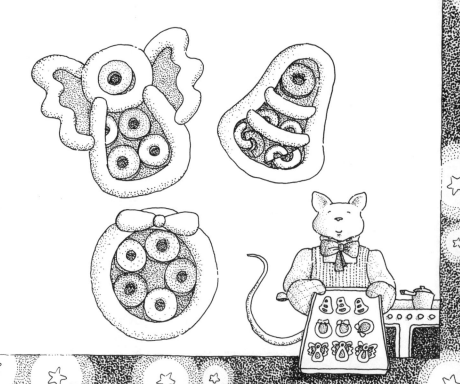

Almost all preschool children love to make noise—the louder, the better. Little children shake, rattle, and bang toys as soon as they are able to grasp objects. Here are two instruments your child will have as much fun making as shaking. Shake the instruments while singing your favorite Christmas songs.

Tambourine

You will need:

two small sturdy paper plates
single-hole punch, six small jingle bells
stapler, gift-wrap ribbon, crayons or markers
six wire twisters or yarn, scissors
small handful of pebbles, old buttons, or paper clips

Hold the two paper plates so they face each other. Punching through both plates at the same time, punch six holes at regular intervals around the rims. Lay the plates face down. Have your child color Christmas pictures or designs on the back of each paper plate. Help your child cut a dozen or more 8-to-18-inch lengths of ribbon. Arrange the ribbons around one-half of the inside rim of one plate and staple in place. Place the pebbles or buttons on this plate. Set the other plate on top with the faces together. Match the holes you punched earlier and staple at 1-inch intervals around the entire rim. Use wire twisters or yarn to attach the six jingle bells through the holes.

Tiny shakers

You will need:

five or six empty 35-mm film containers
masking tape, Christmas wrapping paper
transparent tape, clear adhesive paper
ruler, pencil
small objects, which you will find with your child (see below)

During the holidays, people stock up on film. Ask friends and family members to save their 35-mm film containers for you. When you have about six, decorate them.

Let your child choose six scraps of Christmas wrapping paper. Measure and cut the paper into 4½-by-1¾-inch rectangles. Wrap the paper around the film containers and secure with transparent tape. Cut pieces of clear adhesive paper the same size as the paper rectangles. Wrap these over the wrapping paper. Have a scavenger hunt in your home to find various small objects to put in the film containers. Look for small nuts and washers, paper clips, buttons, tiny plastic blocks, jingle bells, brass paper fasteners, and beads.

Write the name of each kind of object on a small square of masking tape and attach to the bottom of the film containers. Partially fill each film container with a different kind of object. Replace the caps. Play a game by having your child shake each container and guess what is inside. Look at the bottom for the answers. You and your preschool child can have fun shaking these tiny instruments while listening to favorite Christmas music.

ADVENT ALPHABET REVIEW

 **Angel.** An angel told the shepherds Jesus was born.

  Bethlehem. Jesus was born in Bethlehem.

 **Christmas.** On Christmas we celebrate Jesus' birthday.

 **Decorations.** We decorate our homes to get ready for Christmas.

  Elizabeth. Elizabeth was John's mother.

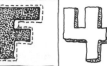 **Four.** During Advent we have four weeks to prepare for Christmas.

 **God** God loved us so much that He gave us baby Jesus.

  Hug. During Advent we can hug people to share our love.

  Inn. Baby Jesus was born in a stable. There was no room in the inn.

 Jesus. Baby Jesus is God's greatest gift to us.

 Kiss. During Advent we can kiss someone on the cheek to show our love.

 Love. We can share our love during Advent by serving others.

 Mary. Mary was Jesus' mother.

 Nazareth. Mary and Joseph's home was in Nazareth.

 Olives. Mary and Jesus ate olives.

 Prayers. We can pray to thank God for sending baby Jesus.

 Questions. Mary had questions after the angel spoke to her.

Ring. During Advent we hear many cheery sounds, like bells ringing.

Shepherds. Shepherds first heard the happy news of Jesus' birth.

Tree. One way we celebrate Jesus' birthday is with a Christmas tree.

Under. The shepherds were watching their sheep under the stars.

Visitors. The shepherds were baby Jesus' first visitors.

Wreath. We light candles on an Advent wreath to help us get ready for Christmas.

XMAS Some people write Xmas instead of Christmas.

YOU God loves you! God has given you plenty of love to share.

Zechariah. Zechariah was John's father.

 MERRY CHRISTMAS

32